Smoke

Alexis Gregory

Performer & Playwright	**Alexis Gregory**
Director	**Campbell X**
Script Consultant	**Rikki Beadle-Blair**
Photography	**Tyler Kelly**
PR	**Chloe Nelkin Consulting**

Smoke was first performed at King's Head Theatre on 2 November 2024.

Alexis Gregory would like to thank:

Bloomsbury Publishing
Deen Atger at Ugly Duck
Robert Chevara
Chloé Nelkin and Gee Carter at Chloé Nelkin Consulting
Reuben Cook
Sara Dawes
Abi Fellows at DHH Literary Agency
James Hogan
Cliff Joannou at *Attitude* magazine
All at King's Head Theatre
Stephen Morris
Night Time Economy
Tom O'Donnell
Mike Robertson
Marc Svensson
Jonny Woo, and John Sizzle, and all at The Divine

King's Head Theatre

King's Head Theatre is a purpose-built, wheelchair-accessible theatre with a 200-seat flexible auditorium and 50-seat cabaret space off Upper Street, Islington which showcases a wide range of performance styles from plays to musicals, to opera and cabaret, to drag and comedy.

Established in 1970, King's Head Theatre was the oldest pub theatre in the UK until it closed its doors in August 2023. For 53 years the theatre was housed in the back room of the King's Head pub on Upper Street in an old boxing ring and pool hall, before opening the new space in Islington Square right behind the pub theatre in January 2024.

Under Artistic Director and Founder Dan Crawford, whose tenure lasted 35 years until his death in 2005, the theatre became known as a breeding ground for new talent and great work. Renowned actors like Maureen Lipman, Hugh Grant, Jennifer Saunders, Dawn French, Alan Rickman and Richard E. Grant all performed at the theatre, and a number of productions transferred to the West End and Broadway, premiering work from writers such as Steven Berkoff, Tom Stoppard, Bryony Lavery and Victoria Wood.

In 2010, the Olivier Award-winning company Opera UpClose Productions became the theatre's resident company for four years, and with Adam Spreadbury-Maher as Artistic Director turned the King's Head into 'London's Little Opera House', winning an Olivier Award for *La Boheme* in the Best New Opera category. Opera remains a key part of the theatre's focus, alongside a commitment to emerging, daring and innovative work, such as *Trainspotting*, the Edinburgh Fringe and touring immersive hit developed by King's Head Theatre.

The theatre showcases a lot of LGBTQ+ work which explores the full spectrum of experiences symbolised by the rainbow flag. It is a home for a new wave of theatre makers, with a focus on work which is joyful, irreverent, colourful and queer.

KING'S HEAD THEATRE TEAM

Executive Producer (Acting CEO) – Sofi Berenger
Producer & Programmer – Zoe Weldon
Technical Manager – Alex Lewer
Theatre Team Manager – Lily Bearwish
Marketing and Communications Consultant – Alistair Green
Development & Community Producer – Elinor Machen-Fortune
Fundraising & Development Associate – Hazel Kerr
Communications & Programming Coordinator – Giulia Lovrecich
Digital, Content & Marketing Producer – Katie Kirkpatrick
Bookkeeper – Alan Mackintosh

Preface by Alexis Gregory

Hot summer. Sat on my doorstep. Writing. Visits from next door's cat. He presses himself against me as I write. Forming Alex's story. His life; fragments of my own, and the lives of others. In *Smoke*, Alex receives a message via his deceased lover's Insta. A hack. On my phone as I write; the real world. Posts about dead gay guys on social media. Comments from online mourners hoping they're 'finally at peace'. We all know what this means. None of us elaborate further. On Insta, after deciding to write this play, I receive a DM 'from' a dead gay guy. You couldn't make this up. I haven't. I knew the guy's face from the clubs, years ago. I'd already made an assumption about his death a few weeks previously. Drugs? Suicide? Suicide because of the drugs? This has been happening for years. Is it happening more now, or do we just hear about these deaths more now? Constant connection. 'What's on your mind?' our devices ask us, and make us expert eulogists. Plenty, if you must know. You *must* know. I write this play quickly / it took me thirty years to write this play. I tell director Campbell X about this project over a video call. Ask him to come on board. He says yes straight away. There is a shorthand between he and I, and others like us. No script yet. Campbell and I on the same (non-existent) page. 'Is it any wonder people like us create their own realities to escape into, where it's safer?', Campbell asks me of Alex, and others like him. Is it any wonder? *Is it?* Campbell and I workshop the script at New Diorama. It's still summer. We work in a beautiful large rehearsal room overlooking the city where Alex, and other men like him, live. There are Alex's in every city. And town. And wherever. The script is long. Too long. I struggle with one particular, heightened, section of the script. I want it to contrast with the realism. Campbell tells me not to force it. I try again with this section the summer after, and the summer after that. It never happens. I'm in a funding loop to get this play on. There is no money. We want to tell this story. Campbell tells me not to worry about the time frame. Any time, is the right time. Today, this feels more so. It feels like we're all slipping. Clinging on. Some of us let go. I'm at a family dinner. I receive texts from my bank about spending that isn't my own. I've been hacked. I receive five hundred emails that night; a known tactic that involves swamping the victim, to bury any real email notifications alerting to unusual activity. I get more text notifications. They are trying to log in from various points around the UK, and from around the world. Organised crime. The hackers spend weeks trying to get into all my social media accounts; my email, my iCloud, my eBay, my PayPal. I manage to keep ahead of hackers, and keep them out of these accounts. At one point, from when they logged into one of my accounts and swapped my mobile number for theirs, to override the identification process, I have one of their mobile phone numbers. My bank reimburses me. It's only a 'lend'. I need to prove a fraud has occurred. I go to the Apple store in Covent Garden. They wipe my iPad. Everything is ok. For now. I become one of those people I'd previously branded as neurotic who don't store any card details online. Never have the same passwords for all your accounts. Turn on two-factor authentication. Be cautious when online out of home and on a public network (I think that's how they got me). Do not click on the link. DO. NOT. CLICK. ON. THE. LINK. I rewrite and rewrite. I go round to friend and collaborator Rikki Beadle Blair's flat. He tells me the script is ready. I feel able to move forward. Another gay guy dies. We used to work in a gay bar together. He and I had chatted online only six weeks previously. I email King's Head Theatre. They come back quickly and say we can put the play on. This story has a home. Then another gay guy dies. I used to see him out and about at clubs, and we worked on a video shoot together. And then another one who I went on holiday with. Then Another One. And Another One. If they're not dying, they're going missing, after walking into the river. We've been dying like this for years. It wasn't meant to be like this. This isn't just about chemsex. This is also just about chems. Niche drugs for niche people. I speak to other queer men. We all say that 'it's complicated' and the reasons are 'a whole other conversation'. Coffee-shop chains tell us love is love, but there is a deficit. As we work on getting this play text ready for publication, I write this preface on my laptop in the gym reception. I write it quickly too. There is no time, and time isn't the same as it used to be anyway. Maybe this piece you're reading now is the piece I struggled to write for three summers. I did it. Now, over to you. Please. I leave the gym. It is a Saturday afternoon. I check my social media. A friend has just been posting about another gay guy who's died. Words of 'finally at peace'. Shorthand. You couldn't make this up. *I haven't.*

Introduction by Campbell X

Smoke makes death, gay men, trauma and social media funny and tender as the main character, Alex, navigates pain. *Smoke* deals with the absurdity of our lives in these turbulent and twisted upside-down times.

When you are fortysomething, like Alex, and have lived through Thatcherism, and been educated under Section 28, to the point where your gay identity was mocked in mainstream culture, surviving to middle-age means all the memories will come crashing back provoked by the death of a loved one. In *Smoke* this causes Alex to be reminded of loving through self-loathing and trauma while he danced in clubs.

We live in a world where the Left is Right, the Right is Might, and the uncertainty of life plays tricks on our mental health. The ground shifts beneath us and Grindr slices and dices our bodies, a meat market for the masses. Yet we still fight to find love by wading through the abundance of flesh.

Smoke is about living in London and trying to connect with other people – even in Acton Town, which *is* indeed far away. We are taken on a journey with Alex who is unravelling because his boyfriend Ben has died. *Smoke* is about dying, even when we are alive. Because to be a femme gay man in twenty-first-century UK is to lose in the stakes of homosexuality. Alex fails and rails against an idealised manhood with biting words, he is a town-crier and truth-sayer in an era of fake news, and false pecs. The 'love that dare not speak its name' is still exiled to No Man's Land. But this time queer culture has exploded online to shout #YesHomo marking our desire on the streets.

'All the world's a stage, / And all the men and women merely players; / They have their exits and their entrances; / And one man in his time plays many parts'; written by William Shakespeare for *As You Like It*, first published in 1623. And here we are 400 years later fulfilling these words but with algorithms like Alex who doom scrolls through mental distress. His scream of consciousness on Instagram live for everyone to participate in and also for him to star in his own story. Warhol was right, and we all now have our fifteen minutes of fame or shame as we document the minutiae of the mundane aspects of our lives.

Smoke is on a physical stage with minimal lighting and production design. *Smoke* strips storytelling down to the word, the voice, the eyes of Alex played by Alexis Gregory who challenges us to look at self before we take that selfie to prove to the world that 'we woz 'ere'. Our digital footprint is fast replacing personal ads, love messages or cries for help previously scrawled on toilet walls.

Why are we losing so many gay men to chemsex and suicide?

By Marc Svensson

'Are suicide and drug-related deaths among gay men becoming normalised?' asks social psychologist and expert in LGBTQ+ mental health Marc Svensson.

That queer people are more likely to have mental health problems and to develop drug addiction and suicidal ideation is well known: an entire social psychological theory was developed to explain it. In 2003, Professor Ilan Meyer, based at UCLA's Williams Institute, published his minority stress theory. It argues that the difference in mental health outcomes between the LGBTQ+ community and the general population can be attributed to the stigma and discrimination we experience because of our minority identity and status.

Since then, numerous research studies have confirmed the validity of the theory by providing consistent evidence that queer people indeed suffer disproportionately from mental health problems. For example, a recent 2024 global study for the LGBTQ+ business community organisation myGwork, which I led in my work as a social psychologist, found that almost half of the 1,000-plus LGBTQ+ respondents had been diagnosed with depression at some point in their lives. However, research on the frequency and cause of suicide, as well as drug-related premature deaths in the community, which often also stem from mental health problems, is much scarcer. More needs to be done to uncover the magnitude of this silent epidemic, and for us as a community to better understand what we can do to stop it in its devastating tracks.

The link between the well-established mental health disparities and premature death rates in our community was given some attention in the mainstream press in 2017, when the *Huffington Post* published a gut-punchingly raw and undeniably accurate examination of what the author Michael Hobbes referred to as 'the epidemic of gay loneliness'. He concluded that despite all the progress towards equality and acceptance of gay people that has occurred over the past couple of decades, gay men were still as unhappy, lonely and disconnected as they had been decades before.

The rise of chemsex

Despite greater equality through legislation and visibility in the media, stigma and discrimination had become more subtle, but no less harmful. Plus, the very fabric of the gay scene had been reshaped by a combination of the rise of online hook-up apps and new sex-and-confidence-enhancing drugs. We had never been more connected, yet feelings of internalised homophobia, stigma and shame pervaded among queer adults, to be inevitably projected onto others. This, Hobbes argued, can create a perfect set-up for drug-induced temporary and shallow connections, most often not lasting beyond a drug-fuelled sex session, commonly referred to as 'chemsex'.

It became more common – and had damaging consequences. Throughout the 2010s, the demand for chemsex support offered by Dean Street, a sexual health clinic in central London, had increased steadily. As did the demand for Antidote, London-based LGBTQ+ charity London Friend's drug harm reduction support service.

In 2019, Channel 4 broadcast *Sex, Drugs and Murder*, a documentary produced by Dispatches in partnership with Terrence Higgins Trust. In it, journalist Patrick Strudwick passionately talks about the common use and too-often deadly consequences of the drugs GHB and GBL (commonly referred to as 'G') on the gay scene. In 2022, GHB/GBL were upgraded to grade B drugs (arguably, primarily because they had become increasingly used as date rape drugs in straight clubs). However, this did not reduce the demand for it on the gay scene – it only made it more expensive.

In July 2018, the government had published a report on the findings of its National LGBT survey alongside an LGBT action plan outlining how to improve the lives of British queer people. Then, in the spring of 2020, the pandemic hit, and everything changed – for the worse.

The lockdown legacy

The pandemic exacerbated many issues that already existed. Loneliness and isolation became an even bigger global problem (not only for queer men), and our mental health deteriorated.

With social-distancing restrictions in place, Dean Street was no longer able to offer face-to-face chemsex support services. Ignacio, one of its former chemsex specialist advisors, decided to set up the charity Controlling Chemsex, offering online support services for people struggling with their drug use and sex addiction. 'People lost their jobs, were banned from socialising, and confined to their homes for months on end, but the hook-up apps were busier than ever,' says Ignacio. 'Many men who contacted us told us their drug use became much more frequent during the lockdown, and almost exclusively associated with casual sex hook-ups.'

Some may argue that normality has somewhat returned, but we are still learning about the long-term effects of the pandemic at societal level, as well as in the LGBTQ+ community. Ignacio explains that the demand for Controlling Chemsex services has skyrocketed, and suicide ideation associated with drug misuse is increasingly common.

Julian Dineen, assistant manager at Antidote, tells me that most of their clients are gay men with crystal meth and/or GHB/GBL addiction. 'The change in drug use, cost and availability has had a significant impact on our community. Chemsex and addiction does not discriminate; it reaches far and wide and impacts the lives of families and loved ones, as well as the individual,' he says.

Crystal meth can significantly impact people's mental health, especially if there is already a pre-existing condition. Low mood, depression, psychosis, suicidal ideation and impaired decision-making are just some of the negative side effects associated with its use. At the same time, GHB/GBL is very dose specific; the margins for error are small and we hear too often about accidental GHB/GBL overdoses.

'It's difficult to really know what's going on without data,' concludes Dineen. 'We can make estimations. We can go on a feel of what we have experienced, but without the data it's really hard to know what's happening and how big the problem is. I certainly have a sense that we're only scratching the surface when we talk about losing loved ones to suicide or a drug-related death.'

Is it an epidemic?

The short answer is we don't know for sure because we simply don't have the data. And that's a central part of the problem. National statistics from England and Wales tell us that men are more likely to end their life than women, and drug-related deaths are most likely to be caused by opiates, and to happen to people born in the 1970s, living in the north of England. In fact, geographically, London has among the lowest rates of drug-related deaths. But are these national statistics also representative of the LGBTQ+ community? As it stands, there is no way for us to know for certain.

Information about sexual orientation is currently not part of the demographic data collected when issuing a death certificate in the UK. Similarly, GHB/GBL – a commonly used drug on the gay/queer scene – is neither included in standard toxicology reports, nor accounted for in national drug-use statistics. GHB/GBL have been linked to many premature deaths on the gay scene, in both accidental and more sinister circumstances.

The logic for not including these drugs in standard toxicology reports is not difficult to grasp. Only a small sub-section of the UK population uses them, and the healthcare system and our government naturally prioritise the drugs causing the most damage across the wider population. However, this leaves the very real possibility that a silent epidemic could be taking place on the gay scene right now, and there would be no way for us to know for sure.

National suicide statistics data comes with a similar limitation in that it does not include information about sexual orientation. It is therefore impossible to know for sure how many more gay/bi/queer men end their lives compared to straight men.

Each person who tragically loses their life prematurely has their own unique story, life experiences and personal circumstances: it's difficult to generalise. It's understandable that family and friends might be hesitant towards the idea of 'reducing' the death of their loved one to a number and a statistic, as a death to be analysed and categorised together with hundreds of other possibly related sudden premature deaths. But it's important that we do, as suicide and drug-related deaths often share many of the same underlying contributory factors.

The lack of reliable data on the occurrence of both types of premature deaths in the gay community is likely one of the reasons why preventative resources and support is so scarce. If we don't know the scale of the problem, how are we expected to develop interventions to prevent them? But this silent killer is far too real to far too many of us.

In the absence of data, we have only anecdotal evidence and research to provide the reasons for an increase in suicide and drug-related deaths in the gay community. Various contributory factors are at play. A lack of self-worth and self-acceptance combined with a sense of loneliness and isolation – a feeling that no one will ever love you for who you really are – are common denominators.

Probing the psyche of gay/bi/queer men, Yale professor and clinical psychologist John Pachankis argues that we experience unique, status-based competitive pressures due to both our social and sexual relationships mostly occurring with other men, who are known to compete for social and sexual gain. He calls it intraminority stress (building on the original minority stress theory) and published a paper with colleagues in 2020 called 'Sex, status, competition, and exclusion: Intraminority stress from within the gay community and gay and bisexual men's mental health'. It suggested that stress from within the gay community due to its perceived focus on sex, status and competition placed gay/bi/queer men's mental health stressors over and above those of traditional minority stressors. In other words, the stress we put on each other within the community can cause more harm to our mental health than the stigma and discrimination we experience from wider society.

However, irrespective of our sexual orientation, we are men living in a heteronormative society that from an early age teaches us to be strong and competitive while hiding our emotions. As most queer men don't go on to form traditional families with children, career and status can become our primary purpose in life. If we then find ourselves not living up to our own – or perceived societal – expectations, we might experience a disproportionate sense of failure compared to men with families and children who contribute to their sense of life purpose. These deep-rooted patterns that affect our ability as adults to create, and believe that we deserve, authentic connections and loving relationships can be unlearned.

Added to the above factors is a learnt avoidance of talking about our emotional struggles, out of fear of coming across as weak or unattractive, while any sense of failure in our professional lives can become overwhelming – to a point where we might find ourselves turning to unhealthy habits to numb the shame or pain.

The stigma and shame often associated with these drug-related accidental deaths is a problem in itself, as it breeds an environment in which the subject is silenced and avoided rather than talked about and properly processed. A disconnect between the family's perception of the life the deceased lived and the life they actually lived might further contribute to a general reluctance to talk openly and honestly about the context in which the death took place, and the underlying factors that might have contributed to it.

The underlying factors behind the high number of premature deaths in our community are complex and multifaceted, and there is obviously no simple magic formula to fix them. However, there are things we can do to face up to this silent epidemic and start tackling the issues.

Firstly, we need evidence that an epidemic of premature deaths is in fact taking place. To do this, we need the data relating to these deaths that is currently not being collected. This is what You Are Loved is about – a new community interest company I have set up to provide spaces for gay, bi and queer men to talk, share and support each other. You Are Loved will launch and run research projects to collect data and develop interventions to prevent suicides and drug-related deaths from happening so frequently in our community.

We also need to get better at celebrating and valuing alternative/queer life course paths. Straight or queer, those who decide to go down the family path will likely associate that with their life purpose. However, those of us who don't necessarily want children need to be reassured that our lives can be just as full of purpose and joy through the pursuit of other paths while finding love and belonging in all kinds of relationships, not only by following heteronormative models, or the temporary sense of belonging 'the gay scene' might provide.

Finally, we need to create more spaces that encourage these authentic connections, to confront and help eliminate the shame, stigma and fear many of us still associate with our sexual orientation. As gay/bi/queer men, we need to learn to appreciate that there is so much more to us than our looks or careers, and that we deserve to be loved and that we belong.

Marc Svensson is a social psychologist and expert in LGBTQ+ mental health. He is the founder of You Are Loved (www.youare-loved.com).

This is an adapted and shortened version of an article which previously appeared in the September/October 2024 issue of Attitude *magazine. www.attitude.co.uk*

Smoke

Character

Alex, *an early-fortysomething gay man.*

Realistically, he could also be played by an older, or younger, actor in future productions of this piece.

Notes

Think of Smoke *as anti-theatre.*

Anti-performance.

Dogma-theatre.

Staged in an empty space.

No set.

Apart from the specified, later, moments of the piece, no lighting design.

The stage fully lit.

One lighting state throughout.

House lights up too.

Everything exposed: Alex and the audience.

Alex can move in and out of, and around, the actual playing space as he delivers the monologue, and speak from any spot in the space.

Smoke *does not utilise any devices or typical conventions that we, as theatre makers, rely on, especially in regards to staging a solo show.*

For example:

The actor never 'becomes' the other characters on stage in a literal way. Such moments are only depicted, in a realistic way, as he may recount an event in everyday life.

The settings and locations do not need to be 'set' onstage; we don't need to see Alex 'move between' them.

This is how I view, and have written for, the 2024 production.

If you're putting on your own future production, do it your way.

If any of the references need updating, do that too.

From the actor playing Alex a naturalistic performance is required.

Matter of fact.

Non-performative.

Conversational.

It should feel like Alex has just walked into the space to tell his story.

Alex addresses the audience throughout.

Alex *enters the space, perhaps through the entrance the audience used.*

He is dressed very plainly: baggy tracksuit bottoms, matched with a simple plain t-shirt, and trainers.

Perhaps the clothes are slightly oversize, and nondescript, and hanging off him.

He heads straight into the centre of the space.

He waits for silence before he starts to speak.

If there isn't silence, he starts with his 'hi's anyway, and gets the audience's attention that way.

Alex
Hi,
hi,
hi.
I'm Alex.
Thanks for being here tonight.
What do I need to tell you about myself?
Ok;
I'm forty-two years old.
I'm a writer from London.
My parents weren't born here,
but I was.
I like the gym;
again,
now that all this is over,
. . . and dogs,
and . . . Mariah Carey.
And . . . I'm here to tell you my story.
It seems strange to call it a '*story*',
because it's the *truth* of what happened to me –

Takes out mobile phone.

– That morning I woke up to a new message on Insta,
from my boyfriend Ben.

By this point Ben had been dead for two years.
Definitely a new message.
Top of my inbox.
DMs officially slid into by my dead boyfriend.
Like many of us,
the first thing I do each morning;
still in bed,
half-asleep,
is check my phone;
check social media,
check the news to make sure the world hasn't caught fire,
flooded,
or frozen over.
That there isn't some new virus,
or pandemic.
That the economy hasn't crashed,
again,
and that we've not gone to war overnight because Putin,
or any of the other maniacs,
have pressed the button.
You know:
all the usual standard fears that we're all navigating.
Ben,
or rather,
his hacker,
messaged me that morning –

He shows his phone again.

– asking me how I am.

He scrolls through on his phone. Finds the message. Reads it out loud.

'Hi Alex,
How r u?' . . .
. . . 'How';
(*spelling out*) . . . letter 'r' . . .
. . . letter 'u'.
No question mark;

which, as a writer, really pissed me off.
Here's the message . . .

He shows a few audience members (three or four people) the message on his phone.

These audience members don't have to be sat closely together; **Alex** *can dart between them, in the space.*

Not just asking me 'How r u' *no question mark,*
but also . . .
. . . using our nicknames for each other,
that only Ben and I knew,
which I'm not going to repeat now because they're
embarrassing,
so whoever's contacted me
has clearly gone through all of mine and Ben's
previous messages.
I can't remember what I first thought when I picked
the message up;
probably 'what the fuck?',
with a question mark,
and then surprise.
And then shock.
And then I was upset.
And really fucking angry;
because I wasn't expecting to see Ben's face,
in his profile pic,
at the top of my inbox,
two years later,
while I'm still trying to . . .
I assume they don't know he's dead,
or else they wouldn't bother messaging me.
I'm not likely to suddenly think my dead boyfriend is
suddenly alive again,
and click on a link they've sent,
or send money,
or pay to get myself back into my own locked account,
or do whatever it is the hacker wants;

we all know people who've been hacked.
And if my dead boyfriend did come back to life,
I'd hope the first thing he'd say to me,
is something other than 'CLICK LINK'.

His phone starts to ring.

He looks at the phone and then looks at the audience.

*He holds the phone out, away from his body as if it is
contaminated.*

*Maybe he places it on the floor and steps away from it, clearly
keeping his distance.*

*He waits for the phone to stop ringing and then, slowly and
carefully, puts it away in his pocket again.*

Did you hear the way the phone rang?
Each third ring was longer than the previous two.

He looks at one person in the audience in particular.

Did you notice?

He looks at someone else in the audience.

I know you did,
because I felt a special connection with you when I first
walked in here tonight.
As if *you know.*
And people like me,
and you,
do know.
After getting the message from Ben;
FakeBen,
I start contacting –

He messages as he speaks.

– our mutual friends to see if they've had a message too.
I say 'mutual friends'.
They were more Ben's friends really.
I never liked any of them.
Basically, they're a bunch of cunts,
and I'm glad I don't have to hang out with them anymore,
and they all turned their backs on me anyway.

He types a message as he speaks.

'Have you had a message from Ben this morning?' . . .
question mark.

He looks at his phone as he surveys the below responses.

Some friends open the message . . .
. . . and ignore it . . .
maybe they think *my* message is fake;
it is,
admittedly,
bizarre;
someone you've not heard from for two years,
getting in touch and asking if you've had a message from
their dead boyfriend.
Or,
they're ignoring my message because they don't want to get
involved again.
And then Jamal,
who Ben used to work with near Carnaby Street;
Jamal is a music journalist;
that's how Ben and I got press tickets to Mariah Carey's
tour,
replies:
'A hack?' . . .
. . . question mark . . .
great; a question mark,
and I message back;

'Of course it's a fucking hack, you fucking moron, Ben's
fucking dead';
Jamal is one of Ben's friends that I *did* like,
but I don't say that.
I say;
'Yeah, def a hack . . . just checking if you got a fake message
too . . . *question mark*',
and Jamal says 'no' and goes offline . . .
. . . and that's if I'm even speaking to Jamal,
and not some actor.
And then Cassie,
who's this really lovely older woman Ben was really good
friends with,
I also became close to her;
the three of us went on holiday together one year,
replies with:

He reads off his phone.

'Alex . . .
are you ok . . .
you know I worry . . .
. . . I've seen your posts on Insta and Facebook' –

Alex *quickly comes off his phone.*

– and I think 'FUCK YOU TOO, CASSIE',
and I never wanted her to come on that FUCKING
HOLIDAY ANYWAY, like a FUCKING GOOSEBERRY,
and then I think about Ben's mum;
Janet,
who's on Instagram,
though she doesn't use it.
Says she's 'crap with technology'.
Janet won't understand a 'hack'.
I think how upsetting it must be;
to have lost a son . . .
. . . and then receive a message from 'him'.

Her bank account got hacked the year after Ben and I got together,
and she cried.
Ben and I helped her get her money back,
but that's not the point;
it's the violation.
Janet's basically my second mum.
Still.
Even with no-Ben.
I used to cut the grass outside her house,
even after Ben died . . .
until she asked me to stop.

He phones Janet and waits for her to answer.

Hi, Janet, it's Alex.
(*Pause.*)
Yeah, *Ben's Alex.*
(*Abruptly, without care.*) Janet, have you had any new messages from Ben?

He puts his phone to his chest and mouths 'fuck' to the audience.

Realises he could have approached this a bit more sensitively.

Returns to the phone call.

Yes . . . *your* Ben,
our Ben.
(*Pause, and then, not unkind.*) Yeah, I know your son is dead, Janet,
trust me,
I know.
(*Pause.*)
No, I'm not.
I told you,
I don't do that anymore.
I've got to go.
I've clearly made a mistake.

He abruptly ends the call.

He looks at his phone in his hand, and then maybe around at the audience members watching him.

What now?

Alex *shrugs.*

Maybe smiles.

Nothing to lose.

FakeBen did ask how I am –

He starts scrolling through his phone.

I don't want to be rude and ignore him.

He replies to FakeBen's message.

He speaks as he types.

'Hi, *Ben* . . .
I'm good thanks . . .
how are you . . .
question mark . . .
. . . long time, no speak' –

He speaks to the audience:

– yeah, two fucking years, because you're fucking dead.

He presses send.

He watches his phone.

By **Alex***'s reaction, we can see that FakeBen is immediately replying.*

Alex *reads the new message out:*

'Hi, Alex,
good to hear from you.

What u up to?'
The letter 'u', still no question mark.
I reply . . .

He types:

'I want to meet you.'

He reads the next immediate response:

He replies . . .
'ok';
not the most enthusiastic response I've ever had to an invite,
but in theory Ben is dead;
I understand he may find it hard to get excited
about things.

He checks his phone again.

'When?' FakeBen's asking.

Alex *speaks as he types:*

– 'Now,' I say.
He comes straight back with 'YES',
. . . in capitals;
Ben never did know how to play hard to get, so he's got
that bit right –

Alex *speaks as he replies.*

– 'Where, *question mark*,' I ask.
'Outside Acton Town tube station,' he says,
and I think who the fuck meets anyone outside Acton Town
tube station?

Alex *speaks as he types.*

'Yeah, great,' I say . . .
'Can't wait,' I say . . .
'Me neither,' he says.

I'm saying 'he'.
Maybe I'm setting up a date with a woman.
First time for everything.

Alex *'speaks' to Ben, placing him high above him in the sky.*

See, Ben, I'm not afraid of trying new things.
He used to say I was,
because I didn't want to go bungee jumping,
or skydiving.
or jet-skiing,
or swim with sharks on that holiday,
or engage in any activity that involved a high risk of death.

He checks his phone.

FakeBen's gone offline.
I'm not stupid.
It's not like he'll turn up today.
I'll be stood there,
at Uxbridge tube station . . . .
or Ealing Broadway . . . .
or wherever the fuck he's sending me,
where the fuck is he sending me?

He checks phone to remind himself.

'Acton fucking Town'.
And if he does show up,
which is unlikely,
he'll be sat across the road,
in a coffee shop,
laughing at me making a total fool of myself.
What am I trying to prove?
That I give a fuck?
To who?
Myself?
Ben?
Ben's dead;

he'll know fuck-all about what does, or doesn't, happen
later today.
Or am I trying to prove something to 'them'?
There could be several of them there,
waiting for me.
A set-up,
An ambush.
It wouldn't be the first time.
I won't live in fear.
Not anymore.
I go to Acton fucking Town tube station,
and it takes forever to get there,
because it's Acton fucking Town,
and I wait,
and I wait . . .
and I'm online –

He pulls out his phone.

– going live on Insta –

He films himself.

– because I'm exposing FakeBen,
and whoever he works for,
to prove to the world what I'm up against.
And then there he is:
FakeBen.
Walking straight towards me.
I know it's him the moment I see him,
because . . .
some of us know.

*Maybe at this point indicates the person in the audience he
'connected' with earlier.*

FakeBen dashes into a mini-supermarket a couple of doors
down from the tube,
one of those small independent ones.

Of course he does;
he didn't expect me to turn up.
I follow him in.
FakeBen is stood towards the back of the store where you go
through to the stock room,
if it even is a real stock room,
if this even is a real shop.
He's talking to a guy who works there.
I get up close to FakeBen,
still filming,
still going live.

He demonstrates his surreptitious filming.

I pretend I'm looking in the fridge;
at the hummus,
and yogurt,
and the crisps.
Why the fuck are there crisps in the fridge?
This is totally not a real shop.
FakeBen's acting like he doesn't recognise me;
carrying on chatting to the shop-guy.
FakeBen leaves the fake shop.
I follow him out.
The other guy;
FakeBen's mate,
who's clearly an actor too,
calls after me:
'Can't find what you're looking for, mate?'
And I say, 'I'm looking for some crisps, *mate*,
but I prefer them at room temperature, *mate* . . .
no offence, *mate* . . .',
and I'm following FakeBen down the street,
still –

He demonstrates filming FakeBen ahead of him in the street.

– live on Insta.
Suddenly we're one,

two,
three streets away,
and I'm thinking how my world has switched;
how I'm doing the following now,
instead of me being followed.
And I'm being pretty obvious about it with FakeBen.
I want him to see me;
like I see 'them' every day;
the guy in the high-vis jacket pretending to empty the
bins,
the FakeMum with no baby in her pram,
strangers filming me just cause I go for my runs at 3 a.m.
Every time FakeBen turns a corner,
I do too;
echoing all his moves.
He's not responding;
he's trained not to.
Probably trying to lead me somewhere to dose me up on
GHB and kill me off like one of those Grindr-gay-serial-
killers that knocks off the fags one by one,
and nobody gives a fuck because it's just Another Dead
Gay.
I know that's the aim:
to be rid of me;
one less gay as a burden on the state.
And then we're at FakeBen's home.
He takes out his key,
goes in,
and just before his front door shuts,
I slide in behind him;
no, not really,
I just wish I did;
so that he'd know how it feels to have strangers in his home;
like I've had in mine,
moving furniture around when I'm out,
once they even took my rubbish out;
which did save me a job to be honest.
I look through the ground-floor window of his flat.

His home looks quite nice, to be fair;
lots of modern art on the walls;
not to my taste;
a bit too 'try hard' if you ask me,
but ok if you're straight,
I guess.
I see him chatting to some girl;
his girlfriend,
at least that's who I assume the bitch is.
I step back from the window,
still in their front garden,
yeah, they've got a front garden,
and probably a back one too;
the flat's the whole ground floor;
open plan;
I can see right through.
In fact, they've probably got the whole house;
three floors plus the basement.
Mummy and Daddy probably helped FakeBen and . . .
Allegra buy it;
because I know her name's Allegra,
or Arabella,
or Clemmie,
and I pick up their wheelie bin just beside me,
and throw it through the window and glass goes
everywhere.
Allegra's screaming;
looking through where the window *used to be*,
at me,
like *I'm the mad man*.
They're both covered in blood;
their own and each other's.
Both staring at me.
They seem kinda shocked to be honest;
weirdly,
and unnecessarily,
freaked out.
I'm still filming –

Alex demonstrates on his phone.

– because if they try and turn this against me in court,
I need evidence to show I was set up;
though I didn't really throw the wheelie bin through the window,
I just wish I had . . .
. . . because they need to know the risk involved in taking the piss out of me;
they need to report this shit back to whoever's in charge.
In reality,
. . . (*To himself.*) ha . . . 'reality',
like most people even know what reality is;
in reality,
through the window,
I see FakeBen and Allegra going about their business;
obviously discussing who they're going to catfish next.
I know she's in on it too.
I walk away to think about my next step.
I go back to FakeBen and Allegra's home the following morning.
He isn't there.
Just her.
I go back the morning after that,
and the morning after that too;
still no sign of him.
Just her.
On the fourth morning,
I see Allegra through the window,
making a breakfast smoothie;
avocado, spinach, honey, lemon . . . and chilli flakes.
Chilli in a smoothie?
This bitch is totally off her head.
Or . . .
just trying to disguise the taste of what's really in her smoothie;
probably adrenaline extracted from kidnapped kids.
I see her on a Zoom call.

For work.
I reckon she's in digital or marketing.
She looks the type.
Clearly being a catfish's accomplice is only her side hustle.
I take a couple of photos through the window –

He demonstrates the quick snapping with his phone.

– as documentation of her suspect behaviour on the Zoom
and with the smoothie.
I start to get hungry myself.
I haven't had breakfast;
I used to go days without food.
Not anymore.
I need to keep my strength up if I'm going to beat Them at
their own game.
I can't see any cafes in the area,
just artisan bakeries and this one guy selling take-out coffee
from an old, converted, red phone box . . .
and what if I need to make an emergency call?
What if they freeze my mobile phone –

Takes out mobile phone again.

– and I feel unsafe,
and need to alert the authorities?
Some people are so selfish.
I can't find any cafes;
. . . just a Starbucks.
I surrender to the concept, and taste, of corporate
commodification;
which basically translates as an overpriced, and overcooked,
cheese and ham toastie,
that's so stale and solid,
I could've lobbed that through FakeBen and Allegra's
window instead of the wheelie bin,
if I really had lobbed anything through their window.
In Starbucks,
FakeBen is behind the counter making coffees.

The catfishing and ripping people off can't be going that
well if he needs another job too.
So this is why I've not seen him for the first four mornings;
he does earlies.
I get in the queue to order from FakeBen.
This annoying gay-boy from behind the counter comes to
serve me instead;
really thin,
face full of make-up,
high-shaped pointed eyebrows,
and this look on his face like he's just smelt something
really bad;
gayer than a unicorn, in a leather harness, at a Dannii
Minogue fan convention.
I point at FakeBen.
'No, I want him to serve me,' I say.
and the DemonTwink gives me this really dirty look,
like I've just broken the news to him that Lady Gaga didn't
throw the first brick at Stonewall.
And then FakeBen is in front of me;
and the DemonTwink,
thank fuck,
pisses off to listen to some Ariana Grande in the back.
'Hi, what can I get you?' FakeBen says.
(*Loaded, and slow, as if the coffee order is code for something else.*)
'A . . . black . . .
Americano,' I say.
And I eyeball him so that he knows I know.
He puts the order through the till.
I pay him.
He asks me what my name is for the cup,
I say . . . . . (*loaded*) '*Alex*'.
I ask him what his name is;
just to fuck with him,
and he looks me straight in the eye,
and says . . . 'Ben';
rubbing my face in it.
'Ben'.

The blender was on in the background,
I couldn't hear what he was saying,
but I know he said 'Ben'.
Not just hacking into my dead boyfriend's Insta,
but blatantly stealing his whole identify.
I say (*loaded again*) 'You . . . look . . . familiar',
he says, 'So do you';
again, I can't hear him over the blender but I know that's
what he said.
'I should look familiar, you tried to catfish me four days
ago,' I say,
but he doesn't hear me over the blender.
But he does hear when I say (*loaded, and slowly*) 'Sorry,
I've got you mixed up with another Ben; my . . . dead . . .
boyfriend';
just to see his reaction.
FakeBen looks at me like I'm crazy,
and moves on to serve another customer.
I take another quick photo of him as he does so –

*He demonstrates surreptitiously photographing FakeBen with his
phone.*

– for when this goes to court.
My coffee arrives.
I look at the Starbucks paper cup.
It says 'Alex' . . .
and . . .
it's underlined.
Underlined!

*He pulls out an old Starbucks cup, quite battered, as if he's been
carrying it around for a while.*

It says 'Alex' on it, and it's underlined.

They never underline the names on the cups in
Starbucks.

He starts showing the cup to audience members, up close, and also looking at and assessing their reactions.

He studies the Starbucks cup closely as if it's a meteor from out of space.

Like I said:
blatant,
mocking me,
with this . . . hidden message,
this . . . threat.
I go back to the Starbucks every morning for the next
four weeks.
If FakeBen isn't on that morning;
. . . I wait until he is.
I film as much as I can –

He demonstrates filming again.

– for my dossier.
Sometimes I film secretly,

He demonstrates filming surreptitiously with his phone.

– and sometimes not . . .

He demonstrates filming with his phone held out far in front of him, rotating in a circle as he does so.

Maybe, demonstratively, giving the whole space the finger at the same time.

NUMBER OF FUCKS GIVEN?
ZERO;
do they think I enjoy being forced to waste my time in a
Starbucks?
The DemonTwink hates it when I'm here for so long,
waiting for FakeBen.
Looks me up and down like I'm making the place look untidy.

Sometimes,
after a while,
it becomes obvious FakeBen is off that day,
but I still stay on-site until they close,
just in case.
I start to understand FakeBen's shift patterns;
6 a.m., 8 a.m., 12 p.m. or 2 p.m. starts.
I stop going in when he's off;
I don't want to look weird.
Sometimes FakeBen looks annoyed that I'm there,
which is understandable;
If I catfished someone,
I wouldn't want them turning up at my place of work,
perhaps telling my manager,
which I wouldn't do to FakeBen;
I'm drawing this out . . .
. . . to make him suffer.
Some of us are chosen to receive.
I have a transmitter in my head.
They placed it here;
embedded it.
It points out things other people –

Maybe refer back to the audience member.

– *most people*,
can't see,
or hear,
or things other people pretend they can't see or hear,
because they think it's easier for them to be ignorant,
but it won't be in the long run,
when the shit hits the fan and society collapses.
I know a few of you here tonight see the extra stuff too.
It's there in front of us all if we pay attention.
Can any of us really say we don't think society,
the system,
is not corrupt?
Look around you.

The police.
Grenfall.
The Post Office.
Our last government giving money to their mates.
The BBC paying paedophiles.
Covid.
The poison vaccine they wanted us all to have.
There's a second device too;
in my throat.
Can you see it?

He opens his mouth, wide for all to see.

He then uses the light on his phone to illuminate the inside of his mouth.

Realising that perhaps not everyone in the audience can see, he starts moving across the front of where the audience is sat, stopping when he gets to various people, to give them a good chance to view his open, illuminated mouth.

After a moment of this:

If I don't act on what the transmitter is telling me,
the second device in my throat,
which is quite far down,
which is why many of you may not be able to see it –

Opens mouth again and points to back of his throat as a reminder.

– gives me an electric shock.

He suddenly reacts as if he received a short, sharp electric shock in his mouth.

That wasn't a real one,
I just wanted to show you what one was like.
In case I get one tonight while I'm here with you all,
and so you'll know what's going on.
The shocks are punishments for telling the truth.

They're not going to be happy about us all here tonight,
about me exposing them to you.
I'm also telling you about the electric shocks in case any of
you ever have one,
because if they come for me,
. . . they will come for you.
The shocks are painful,
obviously,
that's the whole point of an electric shock.
They're normally when I'm least expecting them;
like, when is anyone ever expecting an electric shock in their mouth?
Sometimes they're at night,
when I'm sleeping,
so I don't sleep.
I stay awake.
There are ways to do so.
They pushed me to that too.
I have to be alert.
Sometimes I don't sleep for days because of the fear of the
shocks.

He addresses an audience member.

Actually, what day is it?

If they don't answer, **Alex** *can move on, and ask someone else.*

Seriously, what day is it?

*When he gets the answer from the audience member, he repeats the
day to himself a few times, quickly, testing how the word tastes in his
mouth, e.g. 'Tuesday, Tuesday, Tuesday, Tuesday'.*

I thought it was *(he says what day of the week it really was two
days ago, i.e. if a Friday, he says 'Wednesday'.)*
Ok, not too far off then.
There was a man,
older than me,
an English tutor I saw out of school because I liked writing
so much.

Probably not as old as I thought at the time,
maybe twenty-eight years old;
everyone seems older when you're a kid,
and I *was* just a kid;
eleven years old.
I knew nothing about the world,
about sex,
about being gay.
His name was Phillip Jadeson.

He suddenly gets another electric shock in his mouth.

He has the same response as last time: his head jolts forward.

After a moment:

That was a real one.
They don't like me talking to you,
getting on with you all;
telling you all the truth.

His phone rings.

He looks at it.

Ben's mum.
Fuck.
I hope they haven't hacked her.

After a moment the phone stops ringing.

A bleep.

Voicemail.

Shit, she never leaves messages.

He listens to the message.

She used my nickname.
In the message.
The one only Ben and I knew.

The one the hacker used.

He tries to listen to the message again.

Fuck.
I've deleted it.
It doesn't matter.
I know what I heard.
I know what I know.
She never liked me.
Never thought I was good enough for her son.
Was good enough to cut her grass though, wasn't I?
Haven't I been through enough?
Not just losing Ben;
everything.
Hasn't she been through enough?
Doesn't she have better things to do with her time;
like grieving for her dead son,
rather than punishing me.
What does she get out of this?
Revenge?
Deep down,
she wished Ben had brought a girl home and not me.
She blames me for him dying;
that it was our lifestyle that did it.
Ben didn't like it when I said she'd prefer it if he hadn't
been gay.
He said, 'But she loved it when we took her to the *Priscilla,
Queen of the Desert* musical . . . and she's got all of Will
Young's albums',
but I'm not so sure.
After Ben was . . .
Janet came round and took loads of Ben's things.
Things she should have;
pictures of him as a child;
some of his clothes
. . . . . and his work iPad that had his Insta on it.

I wondered why she wanted that.
She's been planning this since then.
Ben wasn't hacked;
it's not a hack if someone,
Janet,
just logs in.
Acting like she's not technical,
another actor.
Oh God . . .

He steps out of the performance area and vomits just outside of it.

He can head back in as he delivers the below.

Phillip Jadeson,
the teacher I had for those extra lessons,
started phoning me about study-related stuff at first;
new books,
and new writers to keep an eye on.
That was the link,
the shared interest;
his way in.
He was a published author.
I was in awe of him;
in the way any younger person is with an older person
who's successful at something they're into as well.
Maybe the first person to,
demonstratively,
believe in you.

Maybe he is back in the main performance space now.

I'm at Janet's door.
I stink of puke.
I don't care.
This whole situation stinks a whole lot more.
I'm knocking on Janet's door,

well,
banging on it,
and filming with my other hand;

He pulls out his phone to demonstrate.

– another Insta live because people need to know.
Janet's not answering;
of course she's not;
she knows what she's done.
Eventually a light goes on upstairs . . .
. . . and then off again.
She's scared to face me.
She knows I know.
She's seen what I'm capable of;
it was her who called the police when I smashed my flat up,
because she was 'concerned for my well-being'.
What excuse will she have this time?
The light upstairs goes on again.
I shout, 'IT'S ME, ALEX, OPEN THE FUCKING DOOR'.
I see her at the upstairs window.
She disappears.
The light goes off again.
I bang on her front door some more.
It opens.
She's stood there.
She looks terrible.
I mean,
I've got dried vomit down the side of my face,
but she looks way worse than me.
It must be the guilt of what she's done to her so-called
'second' son;
it's taken its toll.
It's written all over her face;
'Alex . . .'
Janet says, and then,
not unkindly,
she says . . .
'again?' . . .

and then,
not unkindly either,
says . . .
'Alex, go home.'
Faking it that she still cares.
Nah;
I know she just wants to get rid of me.
Janet goes to shut the front door on me.
I push the front door open.
It almost hits her in the face.
I wish it had.
She pretends like she's scared of me or something;
another Engineered Actor.
She slams the front door shut.
I spit on it.
Once.
Twice.
Three times.
Over and over.
Janet opens the door again and says:
'Go away or I'll call the police again',
again,
not unkindly.
I'm still spitting at this point.
Not because I don't realise she's opened the door,
but because I want to get it in her face,
her hair,
her eyes,
her mouth.
I always knew she wasn't to be trusted;
the transmitter told me to be careful of her months ago but
I didn't believe it.
Janet shuts the door in my face again;
pretending to be upset because she's covered in my spit;
like big fucking deal.
I hear her go upstairs.
Her bedroom light doesn't go off this time.
She's stood at the window above me,

waiting for me to leave,
like some kind of weird . . . stand-off,
like I don't have the right to challenge her after what she
did to me,
(*shouting up to the window almost*) you stupid cow,
you fucking bitch,
you fucking cunt;
(*back to audience*) I used to cut her grass,
and way better than whoever's doing it now.
I leave,
because I don't want her calling the police again,
or the Hired Actors *pretending* to be the police.
I'd be Phillip Jadeson's,
that teacher's,
guest at book launches.
He'd get free tickets to see writers give talks,
places like the Southbank Centre;
an exciting, proper, grown-up world suddenly open to me.
At these events,
in the dark,
we'd sit next to each other.
He'd get extra close.
His leg touching mine.
His arm,
leaning over the armrest,
onto my side.
The front of his hand touching the side of my forearm.
Just for a second.
Testing the runnings.
One night,
after one of those launches on the way back to Waterloo
station,
he asked me if I had a girlfriend.
I said no;
lots of boys in my class at that time didn't have girlfriends.
Phillip didn't see it like that.
I know he didn't.
I saw a light switch on behind his eyes.

I remember the actual shift in how he saw me.
'This kid's gay . . . this kid's easy pickings.'

He looks around him.

Don't you think it's weird the way they've set up the chairs
in here?

He gestures to the space, and points to a particular area of seating.

How they've got this many seats there,
and this many here?
I know what it means.
And if you all stop and think for a moment,
you all do too.
I go home.
I have Janet's bank card details from when Ben and I
ordered her food over the pandemic;
another thing I did for that ungrateful bitch.
I go online and go shopping with her card.
I buy shitloads of . . . stuff to be delivered to her house.
I want her to have the stress of it arriving,
to wake up to a text from her bank altering her to erratic
spending,
telling her they're frozen her account,
like how I woke up to her fake message from Ben;
yeah lovely Janet who 'isn't technical',
but is able to work her way around her dead son's iPad
when she wants.
I buy,
and send to her house:
six TVs,
a running machine,
a coffee machine,
and a load of toasters;
about thirty of them,
. . . and . . .
a lawnmower,
because I'll be fucked if I'm cutting her grass again.

I pay for them all on her card,
and then I think that's enough for today.
I'll continue tomorrow,
because I'm exhausted.
I'm tired of pretending they aren't getting me down.
They are.
You see this vein that's sticking out of the side of my head?

He approaches an audience member, and points to the side of his forehead.

– That's stress,
from them.
Does that look normal to you?
You see how they're making me ill?
I wasn't ill before.
I am now.
They want me dead.
And when I do die,
I'll come back and haunt them.
Maybe I'm dead already,
and the haunting has already commenced.

He gets out his phone.

This is from my Facebook;
one of my most recent updates.

He reads off his phone.

'Prophets inhale your victimhood. You live in burning
crumbling towers in above-ground bunkers. You trade in
sex-slaves, Covid, paedophilia, shadow-governments, dark-
web rapes, slaughtered Hollywood starlets, elevated incest,
child slaves and imprisoned prophets. Plagues, warrantless
arrests, social passports and secret rings are your
currency and weapons. You are the horror you hope I
forget. This is your personal heaven.'
I say 'it's from my Facebook',

I say 'one of my recent updates'.
It looks like it's from my Facebook.
It looks like one of my updates.
Buy it isn't.
They hack in and post from my account.
Obviously everyone thinks I've written it,
and that I'm the crazy one.
See how they destroy your reputation?
I'm back in Starbucks.
Now I know Janet is the real FakeBen,
I'm going to have it out with *Fake*FakeBen.
Why did he make me think *he* was FakeBen?
What kind of wider plan is he part of with Janet?
*Fake*FakeBen is on shift,
which of course I knew because I'm still all over his shift
patterns.
I get in the queue for a coffee.
He has the nerve to ask me if I want my 'usual'.
I say, 'Why did you lie to me, you cunt . . .
why did you make me think it was you?'
He acts like he doesn't know what I'm talking about;
'Sorry, dude?',
and pulls this ridiculous face,
pretending he's all confused and shocked,
like really bad acting for someone who is supposed to be a
Social Actor.
FakeFakeBen is saying that if I want a coffee,
my usual,
I'll need to watch my language.
I say, 'I don't want to watch my fucking language, you
fucking fuck'.
He says he can 'help me with a nice coffee' but he can't help
me with '*any other problems I'm having*';
all smug like,
superior,
like my problems aren't caused by him and his Associates,
and what's that even supposed to mean anyway;
'any other problems'?

Janet,
and him;
*Fake*FakeBen,
and not having my Ben with me anymore,
are my problems.

He cries for a moment.

And then stops and pulls himself together.

And then that little shit;
the DemonTwink,
comes and stands behind FakeFakeBen.
and says I 'need to quieten down';
apparently I'm being 'aggressive' and 'upsetting the
customers',
and I say to him 'FUCK YOU, I'M NOT AGGRESSIVE,
YOU FUCKING STUPID FAGGOT'.
The DemonTwink tells me to leave the Starbucks.
I say I want to speak to the manager.
The DemonTwink says he *is* the manager.
I think, 'When the fuck did this little bitch get promoted?'
And then the transmitter in my head tells me it was two
weeks ago,
so the transmitter is useful sometimes.
And then the transmitter starts going crazy in my head,
with all this other information,
and dates,
and numbers,
and I tell the transmitter to 'shut the fuck up'.
The DemonTwink thinks I'm talking to him again;
see how none of this is my fault,
and gets even more annoyed with me,
and tells me to leave again.
And then it all becomes even clearer.
They're all in on it.
Not just FakeBen . . . .
but the DemonTwink;
and all the customers in Starbucks too.

I look around and I see the old guy who's always in here.
I remember the time I saw him on the Northern Line one
evening after seeing him in here the same day.
I thought it was weird at the time.
Now it makes perfect sense.
The DemonTwink is shouting at me:
'Get out, get out'
and something about him and his staff 'feeling unsafe'.
I pick up the coffee *Fake*FakeBen made for me;
and I throw it over the counter.
All over him,
and the Demon Twink.
And I know you all probably think I'm going to say
'I didn't really throw the coffee',
but I did.
I wanted to hurt them.
I get out my phone and take more photos;
more documentation to prove what they've driven me to.
The GayDemonTwinkBitchTrollManager,
who by this point
has probably been promoted to Starbucks CEO,
says I've 'just attacked him and his team';
and I call him a 'stupid faggot' again.
And I call *Fake*FakeBen a 'stupid faggot' too,
even though I know he's got a girlfriend,
but that's beside the point really.
I just like how the word 'faggot' tastes in my mouth.
The police arrive.
As well as the supposed attack,
and damage to property;
like Starbucks can't fucking afford it,
I'm arrested for a homophobic hate crime,
and I'm telling them,
how can I be homophobic?
I've got every Mariah Carey single and album on vinyl,
cassette and CD,
including rarities from Japan, South America and every
other major European country;

plus three life-size cut-outs that were for German promo
only;
do I sound like the kind of bitch who's homophobic?
and I'm trying to show them pictures of my Mariah
collection on my phone –

*He pulls out his phone and demonstrates, scrolling through
his phone.*

– as they're putting me into the back of the van.
And now I'm back at the police station,
and the 'officer' behind the counter,
clearly an actor too;
like, do they think I'm fucking stupid,
is like 'Hello, Alex',
and it is nice of them to remember my name here too,
like they do in Starbucks,
and so yeah,
I'm a 'regular' here as well.

He pulls up a seat, and sits in the middle of the playing space.

Or maybe he sits upstage centre, with his back against the wall.

*This should be the first time he has sat down, in this spot, and
addressed the audience, in this way.*

Ben and I met online.
In my bio I've got a line about a dream-lover rescuing me;
it's a reference to a line from a Mariah song.
Ben replied with the next line from the song,
and in his next message,
said that . . . he'd be happy to rescue me.
And so I knew,
immediately,
Ben was a keeper.
We went on a date *first*,
I know,
weird,

to a straight pub,
I know,
even weirder.
We got on,
and spoke about Mariah for most of the evening.
Well, I spoke about Mariah for most of the evening.
He didn't get my 'We Belong Together' reference but I let
that go because I wanted to have sex with him,
and I wanted him to want to have sex with me.
He also said the *Glitter* soundtrack was his favourite
Mariah album,
which I thought was really unimaginative,
as it's such an obvious fan favourite with the 'Justice for
Glitter' campaign,
but maybe he was trying to impress me,
or had even read up on Mariah,
so I let that go too.
I also ignored the fact he kept going to the bathroom in the
pub,
and returning with white powder around his nose,
and on our second date,
in a gay bar this time;
we gave in and succumbed,
he kept disappearing,
and leaving me alone at the table for like twenty minutes at
a time.
He was sneaking out to buy,
and drink,
more alcohol,
and I guess it's safe to say,
that if you're in a bar,
secretly sneaking out to drink,
there's a problem.
I ignored that too.
I don't want to throw Ben under the bus,
. . . he's not here to defend himself,
but I wasn't into the drugs until I met him.
Ben got me into them;

I'd smoked a bit of weed at festivals,
but that was it.
Cut to,
he and I,
on a Tuesday afternoon,
smoking crystal meth in that alley way in Soho;
you know;
the one with the changing coloured lights between Berwick
and Brewer Street.
And now Ben's gone,
and I'm left smoking it alone,
at night,
to stay awake,
so *that I can be alert for the next fucking electric shock*,
so you see,
none of this is my fault.
Janet,
Ben's mum,
blamed *me* for getting *Ben* into the drugs.
The drugs damaged my head.
Or maybe my head was already damaged and that's what
drew me to the drugs.
I ended up doing drugs everyday,
at work;
I was office temping between writing gigs.
Once my line manager heard me doing coke in the toilet at
work,
and so I knew I had to set some boundaries,
so I only did coke at work when I knew he was definitely off,
or out at meetings.
I also laughed when he caught me doing coke,
because I said to him 'I thought you were supposed to be
my *line* manager',
but he didn't think it was funny.
While Ben was alive,
all of our friends,
who I met via Ben,
who I don't see anymore,

were heavily into the drugs too.
It was everywhere.
There was Pablo;
who was so high one morning,
he jumped on the tube tracks and shut down the whole
Northern line . . .
well not the *whole* Northern line,
just the Bank branch.
And Lewis who took loads of G at work,
and went to Pret a Manger;
the small one on Tooley Street opposite London Bridge
station,
and passed out,
and people took pictures,
and put them on social media.
He lost his job.
He worked in PR for a pharmaceutical company,
so the optics weren't great.

He stands up.

You're probably all wondering how Ben died.
People always want to know.
You must too.
You've all paid to come here;
to watch . . .
to listen.
You must all want your money's worth now that I've started.
I'm stood in front of you;
I must *want* to tell you.
You assume it was the drugs,
now you know he was into them;
another dead gay guy from an overdose,
or suicide because of the drugs.
I assume those things too;
every time I see an announcement on social media about
another beautiful,
young,

dead gay guy,
. . . like Ben,
because Ben was beautiful.
We hear about more deaths now than we used to don't we?
We're in each other's lives for longer,
and more.
now;
with social media.
Previously,
we'd just lose touch with certain people.
Now we're connected,
but separate,
. . . forever.
And I'm queer,
so I see a lot of announcements about other dead gay men.
Ben's death was all over social media.
There were comments and 'thoughts and prayers',
and broken heart,
and crying face emojis,
and then . . .
after a couple of days . . .
it all died down,
and the world moved on,
because it has too.
I was unwell . . .
in case you haven't noticed.
I was sectioned after Starbucks-homophobic incident-
Demon Twink-gate,
. . . *again.*
Janet,
Ben's mum,
paid for my treatment,
again.
I hope I don't let her down,
again.
She says she's forgiven me,
again,
even for the twenty-four toasters I sent to her house,

which she,
very sweetly,
said was only annoying because she'd given up bread
at the time.
She still says I'm still her second son.
She also said she has no idea what Ben's nickname
for me was,
but everything was crazy at that point.
I bumped into Phillip Jadeson;
my old English tutor,
about six months ago,
in the Sainsbury's on Upper Street.
I said, 'It's Phillip, isn't it?,
he said 'yes'.
I said, 'It's Alex . . .
from your writing class.'
He didn't remember me,
or *said* he didn't remember me.
I said . . . 'We used to speak on the phone . . . *for hours* . . .
and hang out at the Southbank Centre . . . *for hours* . . .
. . . the book launches.
. . . *and evenings at your house.'*
He looked through me;
obviously I look different now,
I'm a man now,
but still . . .
no recognition what so ever?
He said he 'couldn't place' me,
and that he 'taught many young people over the years',
and I thought, 'Yeah, and there must have been many,
many *teenage boys* over the years,
and at your house too,
if you can't remember us all',
I said,
'You made me ill',
but he misheard me,
and said he was pleased to see I'd recovered from 'whatever
it was'.

He walked away.
It's easy for him to do so.
His name isn't Phillip Jadeson by the way.
I changed it for you all.
To protect him,
still.
I went back to the Starbucks to apologise to *Fake*FakeBen.
I asked him what his real name is,
he said 'Cameron'.
I asked him what his girlfriend's name is,
he hesitated;
probably wondered why I was asking,
and then probably too scared to not tell me,
he said her name's . . .
'Allegra' . . .
. . . no, not really;
her name's 'Beth'.
I apologised for my behaviour.
He shrugged and said 'it's cool man',
and added,
'we see it all in here',
which really didn't make me feel any better.
He remembered my name,
and what my 'usual' was,
and insisted on giving it to me on the house,
in a paper cup,
with my name written on it,
underlined,
which is all good now,
like totally unproblematic,
with an added 'Please don't throw me' written on the
paper cup,
with a little winking face drawn on too,
which I thought was pretty inappropriate,
considering my history,
but I haven't really got a leg to stand on re 'inappropriate',
have I?
The DemonTwink was on too.

I apologised to him as well.
I asked his name too;
considering it seems to be the theme of the day.
He said 'Davey';
such a twink name.
Though he's not as twinky now.
I didn't recognise him at first.
He's been working out;
you know what it's like when you're young and slim and hit
the gym for the first time,
there's all those sudden changes to your body.
His eyebrows didn't seem so crazy now either.
No make-up.
Even some facial hair.
He looked. . . more grown-up,
and handsome.
He said he didn't recognise me either;
that I look less . . . angry,
and younger,
which is probably the same thing.
He and I are going on a date next week.
He invited me to a Mariah Carey drag night.
Aurelio Sanchez,
this kid from Instagram,
is in the country,
at Two Brewers.
He does her so well,
even I can't tell sometimes.
I think Davey's trying to impress me,
like Ben did with *Glitter*,
the Mariah album . . .
He'll be the first guy I've gone out with since Ben.
I never thought I'd end up with a younger guy,
but everyone's younger than me now,
and anyway,
lots of things I never thought would happen did,
so a date with the DemonTw–
with Davey,

is the least of my worries.
Pookey was Ben's nickname,
his pet name.
I told you it was an embarrassing one.
Ben went missing.
And then he was . . . *found*.
People wonder if it was an accident or intentional.
I wonder too.
I think it was both.
I miss Ben a lot,
of course.
'Something' happened when we got together,
the good stuff;
the. . . magic,
and the other stuff,
the madness . . .
and the moment we let the other stuff in,
it took over and there was no turning back.
Certain things don't matter anymore;
'whose' fault it is;
who got who into the drugs,
if either of us even got the other one into them at all,
if that's even possible.
I'm working through a lot.
I'm not proud of what I did.
I'm ashamed,
but I'm working through that too.
I know the old man in Starbucks wasn't following me
on the Jubilee line.
The guy in the shop,
in Acton fucking Town,
wasn't 'in' on anything;
though I still think it's weird the crisps were in the fridge.
I know there was no transmitter in my head.
Or device in my throat.
But it felt like there was.
Because there *was* actual,

physical,
pain shooting through me;
but that pain was the result of something else within me
already.
I find joy elsewhere now.
In the everyday.
You have to.
It really is the simple things;
being sat outside a coffee shop in Soho at 9 a.m. on a
Monday morning,
and *not* still being up from the night before.
Today,
seeing a little kid,
a little boy,
and his grandmother I assume,
sat opposite me on the tube,
sharing a joke,
and laughing like decades-long old friends;
not a care in the world.
Both of them,
privately hysterical.
And on the way here tonight,
I had to go through Covent Garden,
via some back street by the Opera House,
and I heard the most amazing soprano,
warming up,
from an open window above me,
hitting these crazy notes,
and it was magic.
It's there if we let it find us,
if we look for it;
like I looked for everything else before.
I need to thank FakeBen,
whoever,
wherever,
whatever,
FakeBen is.

They did help me;
by being what finally made my life fall apart for the
last time,
I hope;
one day at a time.
People often ask me about the 'message' from Ben,
FakeBen,
if it really existed?

The lights change.

The playing space is suddenly swamped with one really bold colour,
perhaps purple, electric blue, or red, etc.

At the same time we lose the house lights.

One.
Yes, there was a message 'from' Ben's account.
A regular everyday hack that I overreacted to.
If I'd ignored it,
or simply reported the account,
I'd have been ok.

The lights change colour again, to a different, bold colour.

Two.
There was no message at all.
It never existed.
I imagined it all.
It was a delusion.
Part of my psychosis.
I know I showed you –

He points at one of the audience members he showed the message to
earlier.

– the message, and you –

He points at another audience member he showed the message too.

– but you only saw it very briefly,
it could have been any,
existing,
regular,
message in my inbox.
It's easy to see what your brain is telling you to see,
when it's wrapped up in a whole lot else.
I got it wrong.
If I can imagine an electric device in my mouth,
I can imagine a message on Insta.
I got caught up in *something* . . .

He looks around him, and takes in the audience.

. . . maybe we all did.

The lights change colour again, to a different, bold colour.

Three.
There was a hack.
But they've removed the thread from my inbox.
This is why I can't view it anymore . . .

He pulls out his phone, and starts scrolling through.

– Another trick to control me,
and make me –

He gestures to the audience again.

– and everyone else,
think I'm crazy.
No –

*The light snaps off and we return to our general ('no lighting')
state.*

House lights back up too.

– No.

He stops in his tracks.

He realises he can't put himself through this again.

He says the below almost to himself.

There was no message.
I'm better now.
There was a hack though.
Not in the conventional sense.
My life was cut open.
By me.
By the world.
Maybe it was easier to think it was via some imaginary
message on Ben's Insta.
I'm better now.
I want you all to know.
I want everyone to know.

He steps out of the main performance space.

*He heads to another spot, maybe a corner, or near the wall, towards
a second mobile phone, on a stand, that has been filming the
whole time.*

He picks it up, and heads back to the centre of the space.

He looks into this phone, right down the lens.

*Maybe he takes the original mobile phone out of his pocket, and
holds it, or places it on the floor, so that it is clear there are two
separate devices.*

He speaks into the second mobile phone on the stand.

Maybe sharing this will help;
I shared all the other stuff online.
(*To audience.*) People will understand.
They'll want me again.
(*Down lens of phone again.*) You'll want me again.

He presses a button on his phone to share.

He steps back and looks at his phone on the stand.

Snap to black.

Audio recording: the sound of a soprano singing, hitting epic high notes.

Curtain.

Discover. Read. Listen. Watch.

A NEW WAY TO ENGAGE WITH PLAYS

This award-winning digital library features over 3,000 playtexts, 400 audio plays, 300 hours of video and 360 scholarly books.

Playtexts published by Methuen Drama, The Arden Shakespeare, Faber & Faber, Playwrights Canada Press, Aurora Metro Books and Nick Hern Books.

Audio Plays from L.A. Theatre Works featuring classic and modern works from the oeuvres of leading American playwrights.

Video collections including films of live performances from the RSC, The Globe and The National Theatre, as well as acting masterclasses and BBC feature films and documentaries.

FIND OUT MORE:
www.dramaonlinelibrary.com • @dramaonlinelib

Methuen Drama Modern Plays

include

Bola Agbaje
Edward Albee
Ayad Akhtar
Jean Anouilh
John Arden
Peter Barnes
Sebastian Barry
Clare Barron
Alistair Beaton
Brendan Behan
Edward Bond
William Boyd
Bertolt Brecht
Howard Brenton
Amelia Bullmore
Anthony Burgess
Leo Butler
Jim Cartwright
Lolita Chakrabarti
Caryl Churchill
Lucinda Coxon
Tim Crouch
Shelagh Delaney
Ishy Din
Claire Dowie
David Edgar
David Eldridge
Dario Fo
Michael Frayn
John Godber
James Graham
David Greig
John Guare
Lauren Gunderson
Peter Handke
David Harrower
Jonathan Harvey
Robert Holman
David Ireland
Sarah Kane

Barrie Keeffe
Jasmine Lee-Jones
Anders Lustgarten
Duncan Macmillan
David Mamet
Patrick Marber
Martin McDonagh
Arthur Miller
Alistair McDowall
Tom Murphy
Phyllis Nagy
Anthony Neilson
Peter Nichols
Ben Okri
Joe Orton
Vinay Patel
Joe Penhall
Luigi Pirandello
Stephen Poliakoff
Lucy Prebble
Peter Quilter
Mark Ravenhill
Philip Ridley
Willy Russell
Jackie Sibblies Drury
Sam Shepard
Martin Sherman
Chris Shinn
Wole Soyinka
Simon Stephens
Kae Tempest
Anne Washburn
Laura Wade
Theatre Workshop
Timberlake Wertenbaker
Roy Williams
Snoo Wilson
Frances Ya-Chu Cowhig
Benjamin Zephaniah

For a complete listing of
Methuen Drama titles, visit:
www.bloomsbury.com/drama

Follow us on Twitter and keep up to date
with our news and publications
@MethuenDrama